First published in 2011 by Wayland

Copyright © Wayland 2011

Wayland
338 Euston Road
London NW1 3BH

Wayland Australia
Level 17/207 Kent Street
Sydney, NSW 2000

Commissioning editor: Camilla Lloyd
Designer: Emma Randall
Picture researcher: Shelley Noronha

Picture Acknowledgments: The author and publisher would like to thank the following for allowing
their pictures to be reproduced in this publication: Cover and 16: Getty Images; throughout background:
RedShineStudio/Istockpoto; 1, 2 100 words/Shutterstock; 5, 11, 25, 26, 27 Getty Images; 6, 20 Bloomberg via Getty
Images; 7, 10 Roger Ressmeyer/Corbis; 8 SSPL via Getty Images; 9 The Image Works/Topfoto; 12 Sipa Press/Rex
Features; 13 Snap/Rex Features; 14 Time & Life Pictures/Getty Images; 15 AFP Getty Images; 17 Monica M.Davey/epa/
Corbis; 18 Imaginechina/Corbis; 21 Xinhua/Photoshot; 22 Yi Lu/Corbis; 23 Lai Xiangdong/Xinhua Press/Corbis; 24
WireImage/Getty; 30 Ivan Stevanovic/Istockphoto; 32 Chris Hutchison/Istockphoto. Every attempt has been
made to clear copyright for this edition. Should there be any inadvertent omission please apply to the
publisher for rectification.

British Library Cataloguing in Publication Data:
Sutherland, Adam.
Apple. -- (Big business)
1. Apple Computer, Inc.--Juvenile literature. 2. Computer
industry--Juvenile literature.
I. Title II. Series
338.7'62139-dc22

ISBN: 978 0 7502 6428 0

Printed in China

Wayland is a division of Hachette Children's Books, an Hachette UK company.

www.hachette.co.uk

Contents

An Apple in every home

Apple is flying high. The company that invented the personal computer has successfully branched out into music and telecommunications. Today there are 50 million iPhone and iPod users, over 500 million active iTunes users worldwide, and sales of the iPad, Apple's flatscreen 'tablet' PC, reached 7 million by the end of 2010, with 57 million sales per year estimated by 2015.

With revenues of $26.7 billion (£16.4 billion) in 2010, Apple is now the largest mobile-device company in the world and its shares are worth roughly 43 times their level of ten years ago.

The iTunes Store has even overtaken America's largest supermarket chain Wal-Mart to become the largest retailer of music in the USA.

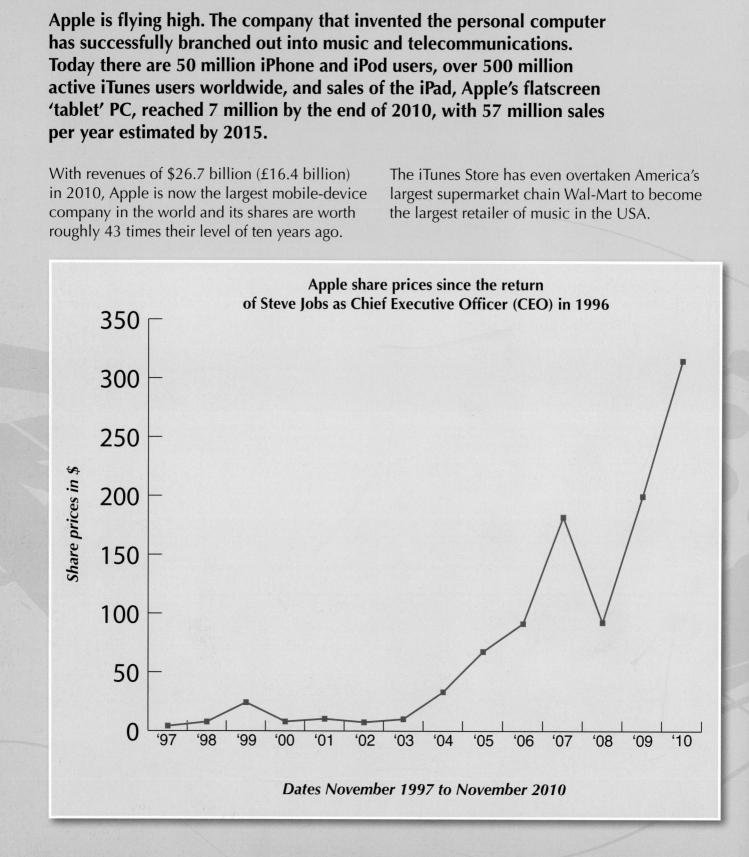

Apple share prices since the return of Steve Jobs as Chief Executive Officer (CEO) in 1996

Share prices in $

Dates November 1997 to November 2010

But Apple's story, similar to the story of one of its founders Steve Jobs, is full of downs as well as ups. Apple's skill has always been innovation. They created the world's first truly personal computer, the Apple II, in 1977 and made groundbreaking machines that the industry loved, and that consumers wanted to have in their homes. But somewhere along the line the focus got lost, and the company started to fall behind more business-oriented companies like IBM and Microsoft in the race to put computers on every office desk in the world.

Steve Jobs was forced out of Apple, and ended up turning Pixar (an animation company) into the most successful and well-respected computer animation studio in the world! Steve never lost his love for Apple, however, and eventually returned to the company in 1996 to start an incredible phase of growth and success that is still going to this day.

In the following pages, you will read about the founding of Apple, the machines they have produced, and the decisions they have made – good and bad – that have created the Apple that we all know today. Along the way, you'll discover more about the years of development that go into creating great products, and the inspired business planning that has helped Apple expand into new markets, stay one step ahead of the competition and, most importantly, stay on top.

> ❝ I was worth over a million dollars when I was 23, and over ten million dollars when I was 24, and over a hundred million dollars when I was 25, and it wasn't that important because I never did it for the money. ❞
> **Steve Jobs**

The origins of Apple

Apple was founded in April 1976 by Steve Jobs and Steve Wozniak. The pair met in 1969 when Jobs was still in high school, and Wozniak – known as 'Woz' – was working at computer company Hewlett-Packard and had a reputation as the local electronics whizkid. 'He was the first person I met who knew more electronics than I did,' Jobs remembers.

In 1960s Silicon Valley, it was cool to be into electronics, and the two men became regulars at a local computer hobbyists' group called the Homebrew Computer Club. Woz would pick up ideas at meetings, then go home and work on them so he could impress his fellow 'techies' at the next gathering. He enjoyed doing things better, with fewer parts and more elegant engineering, than anyone believed possible. If Woz had the know-how, Jobs had the get up and go. When he had an objective, nothing stood in his way of reaching it.

▼ *Steve Jobs launching the iPad in 2010 in the foreground with a picture of him and co-founder Steve Wozniak in the background.*

This picture shows Steve Wozniak in 1984. Woz left Apple in 1987, but remains a shareholder in the company. In September 2000 he was inducted into the National Inventors Hall of Fame.

In 1975, the world's first 'personal computer', the Altair, was launched. It came in kit form and, once constructed, just lit up a line of bulbs when you entered the correct – and complicated – binary codes. It was an electronic breakthrough, and Jobs started planning how they could profit from this new field. Jobs and Wozniak formed a company and named it Apple Computer – partly because of Jobs' love of pop music (the Beatles' record label was also called Apple), and partly because 'Apple' would come before 'Atari' – Jobs' former employer – in the phone book.

Woz started building circuit boards that hobbyists could then load up with components to create their own basic computer. The plan was to build these boards for $25 (£16) each, and sell them on for $50 (£32). Instead, they were persuaded by local computer store owner Paul Terrell that they would do better business if they produced and sold ready-stocked boards. These boards – Apple's first product – were called Apple I. Terrell's Byte Shop ordered 50 at $500 (£320) each – a first order worth $25,000 (£16,000). Apple was on its way!

Brains Behind The Brand

Steve Wozniak – co-founder of Apple

Computer engineer Steve Wozniak – known as 'Woz' – is often credited as the person who started the personal computer revolution. His Apple II design, introduced in 1977, brought computers onto the desks of ordinary people. Sold as a finished computer, rather than as a kit, it was accessible to the mass market rather than just to hobbyists and fellow engineers.

A plane crash in 1981 left Woz with significant memory loss, and although he returned to work in 1983, he was no longer active in new product development.

> "Steve Jobs didn't really set the direction of my Apple I and Apple II designs but he did the more important part of turning them into a product that would change the world."
> **Steve Wozniak**

By the end of 1976, Apple had sold 150 of Apple I, representing nearly $100,000 (£64,000) in revenue. Woz was making nearly as much money from Apple as he was from his day job at Hewlett-Packard, but still he wasn't ready to commit himself to Apple full time.

However, he was committed to improving on his own Apple I design. The Apple I was a fully assembled circuit board containing about 60+ chips. However, to turn it into a working computer, users still had to add a case, a power supply, a keyboard, and even a monitor. Woz soon followed the Apple I with the Apple II, single-handedly designing all its hardware and software – an extraordinary feat for the time. And what's more, he did it all while working at his day job at Hewlett-Packard!

The Apple II came as a finished product, rather than as a kit, with a built-in monitor, keyboard, sound and high-resolution graphics. Presented to the public in 1977 at the first major computer trade show in California, the West Coast Computer Faire, it was the first computer designed for the mass market, not just for engineers and computer 'nerds'.

Around the same time, Steve Jobs saw an ad campaign for electronics company Intel. Rather than focus on the science, the ad used poker chips, hamburgers and racing cars to explain how great Intel was. Jobs tracked down the man who dreamed up the ad, Regis McKenna, and refused to leave his office until he took on Apple as a client!

McKenna and Jobs both agreed that the key to the company's growth was in reaching beyond the hobbyist market, and selling the idea that 'computers are for everyone'. It's an idea that Apple still uses successfully to this day.

◀ *The revolutionary Apple II was the first computer to be sold as a finished product.*

▼ *The Apple computer store in Tokyo, Japan shows the familiar Apple logo.*

Brains Behind The Brand

Susan Kare – graphic artist at Apple

Susan joined Apple in 1982 and originally worked in the Macintosh software team, designing fonts and user interface graphics – the icons that appear on your computer screen depicting everything from the hard disk to the waste basket. Her most recognisable works from her time with Apple are the Chicago typeface (used on the first four generations of the iPod), the Geneva typeface, and the Happy Mac symbol (the smiling computer that welcomed Mac users when they started their machines).

Business Matters

Branding — all the qualities and features of a product, including its name and its appearance, are presented to the customer as a brand. To be successful, all brands — from Apple to McDonald's to Nike — need to be distinctive (stand out in some way from competitors), consistent (always provide the same level of quality, and therefore be seen as reliable), recognisable (through a logo or 'look' of a product) and attractive. Everyone recognises Apple's half-eaten apple logo!

Fallout at the top

Helped by several innovative software programs, including the first accounting spreadsheet Visicalc, the Apple II became a huge seller, and Apple became the world's number one personal computer company. By 1980 they had grown to 1,000 employees and had manufacturing plants as far apart as California, Ireland and Singapore.

In December of that same year, Apple shares went on sale on the New York Stock Exchange in a process called an IPO (which means 'initial public offering'). The 4.6 million shares were sold within one hour, in the most successful IPO since the Ford Motor Company in 1956. Overnight, Steve Jobs was worth $217.5 million (£138 million), making him one of the USA's richest men.

Steve's passion and drive for excellence meant that he worked his employees hard. He earned $250,000 (£160,000) per year in salary, but insisted that each of his engineers earn no more than $30,000 (£19,000) – they were the lowest paid engineers at Apple – plus he expected his

team to work 80-90 hours per week. Steve was trying to ensure that his engineers really wanted to work for Apple rather than to make a lot of money. Most still loved him for his genius, and desperately wanted to work on Steve's projects.

However, Steve went on to make several expensive mistakes – new computers like the Apple III, and the high-powered business machine the Lisa, both flopped, and the first Macintosh, which was meant to save the

▼ *The Lisa featured a detachable keyboard, mouse and graphical user interface. Its high price meant it was not a market success.*

Mike Markkula with the first Apple II computer and its carrying case in 1977. ▼

the company, could only generate 10 per cent of the sales that Steve had predicted. Customers complained about the lack of software programs, the shortage of memory, and the small screen. Steve was getting wrapped up in design, and forgetting to give the customers the functions that they wanted.

Apple sales stalled, the company announced a financial loss, and share prices fell as a result. The Apple board of directors acted quickly, removing Steve from his position as chairman, and putting John Sculley (former head of Pepsi) in his place. Steve resigned from the company he founded on 28 May 1985.

Brains Behind The Brand

Mike Markkula – former CEO of Apple
Steve Jobs convinced Mike of the huge potential market for the Apple II and personal computers in general.

Mike provided important managerial experience and support for the new company, along with a $250,000 (£160,000) investment, and became a one-third owner of Apple, and employee number three. Mike brought order and structure to the young company, hiring Apple's first president, Michael Scott, and serving as chairman himself from 1985 until 1997. Steve Wozniak credits Mike – even more than his own innovative computer designs – for the long-term success of Apple.

Business Matters

Company directors – these people, often called a board of directors, oversee the activities of a company. A board's role is determined by the powers and responsibilities granted to it by a company's own rules and regulations. These rules usually cover the number of members of the board, how they are chosen, and how often they meet. The board usually chooses one of its members to be the chairman. Typical duties of a board include: setting the rules that run the organization; selecting, appointing, supporting and reviewing the performance of the CEO; approving annual budgets; reporting to shareholders on the company's performance.

Steve returns to Apple

After Steve's departure from Apple, he sold all but one of his shares. He used the money to form NeXT, a computer development company specialising in the higher education and business markets. He also bought special effects and computer animation company Pixar (originally called Industrial Light and Magic) from Star Wars director, George Lucas.

Through NeXT, Steve was learning valuable lessons about the importance of balancing hardware (a computer's outer look and feel) and software (what it actually does). At the same time, he was turning Pixar from a company that lost $1 million (£630,000) per month into Hollywood's most respected and successful computer animation studio. Steve's biggest success came when Pixar agreed a distribution deal with Disney, and the first film they co-produced was the hugely successful *Toy Story*!

Meanwhile, Apple was struggling. Computers from its main competitor IBM, powered by Windows software produced by Microsoft, were used in virtually all businesses around the world. Steve's successor John Sculley had been unable to improve Apple's fortunes. While he was chairman, their market share (the percentage of computers they sold compared to every other company) fell from 20 per cent to just 8 per cent. Apple directors started to look around for someone to buy the company. Revenues were so low, that no one was interested!

Instead, Apple hired a new chairman, Gil Amelio, former president and CEO of technology company National Semiconductor. One of the first calls Gil received was from Steve Jobs. Steve told Gil that as the company's co-founder, he was the only person that could put Apple back on track.

Eventually, Steve got his wish. In 1996 Apple were searching for a new operating system to power their next wave of computers, and Steve persuaded Gil to buy NeXT. In exchange for $377.5 million (£240 million) and 1.5 million Apple shares, Gil acquired all Steve's 300 staff and his NeXTSTEP software system. The financial figures for 1997 showed that Apple sales had fallen to $7 billion (£4.45 billion), and losses were over $1 billion (£640 million). The board asked Gil to step down, and appointed Steve Jobs as CEO!

← *Gil Amelio, CEO of Apple in 1996.*

▼ *The first* Toy Story *film was released in 1995.*

Business Matters

Mergers and acquisitions — this phrase refers to the aspect of company strategy and finance that deals with the buying, selling and combining of different companies. This strategy can help a company grow rapidly within its market without having to create another separate company. An acquisition is the purchase of one company by another company, as when Apple bought NeXT. A merger is when two companies combine to form a third, new company.

> Getting fired from Apple was the best thing that could have ever happened to me. The heaviness of being successful was replaced by the lightness of being a beginner again... It freed me to enter one of the most creative periods of my life.
>
> **Steve Jobs**

Riding the Internet wave

Steve was back at the company he loved, but there was no time to celebrate. Apple was in trouble and he needed to act quickly. One of Steve's first calls was to Bill Gates, the owner of Microsoft. The pair quickly struck a deal.

In exchange for investing $150 million (£95 million) in Apple, Microsoft would produce and sell Microsoft Office products for the Macintosh. Apple would also install Microsoft's Internet Explorer Web browser on all Macs sold. Apple fans booed the announcement at the MacWorld exhibition in Boston in 1997, but Steve knew that without market leader Microsoft's support, Apple was in real danger of becoming irrelevant and outdated.

Steve was probably the only man who could bring order to the chaotic corporate culture that he had created when he formed Apple. He cut back on company spending – axing 70 per cent of new products in development, putting a stop to expensive business class travel for employees – and replaced the whole board of directors who had employed him!

By January 1998, Apple was back in profit – even though sales had fallen slightly to $5.9 billion (£3.75 billion) – and by January 2000 the company's market value had risen from $2 billion (£1.3 billion) to over $16 billion (£10 billion).

The board granted Steve $870 million (£550 million) worth of Apple stock for his efforts, and his own Gulfstream V corporate jet.

But what was next? Steve was convinced that he needed to catch the start of the Internet wave. If he could combine the freedom of the Internet with the simplicity and great design of the Mac, he was sure it would be a winning combination. The result was the iMac, a combined monitor and hard drive with funky coloured plastic side panels that sold for $1,300 (£830) and came loaded with everything you needed to go online. 'Plug and play' was the concept – open the box, plug it in, and get surfing! The idea was revolutionary – and Apple sold two million iMacs in just over a year.

Another of Apple's innovations was the iBook, an iMac-inspired laptop, which offered something called 'Airport' – the ability to connect wirelessly to the Internet. Other companies were offering this, but Apple made the most noise about it, and it worked. Apple was back on top.

◄ *Steve Jobs launches the iBook in 1999.*

Brains Behind The Brand

Steve Jobs – chairman and CEO of Apple
Steve Jobs is one of the world's best known and well-respected businessmen. Steve co-founded Apple in 1976, and 20 years later returned to turn around its fortunes. As Apple's CEO, it is Steve's job to develop company strategy, and make sure everyone within Apple follows it.

A CEO's main roles are to facilitate business outside of the company, and to guide employees towards clearly defined objectives. For example, Steve wanted to expand Apple beyond a computer company, and make it an entertainment company. He gave new directions to research departments to focus on music, and then telecommunications, and hired new specialised employees where necessary to get the job done.

> *Innovation distinguishes between a leader and a follower.*
> *Steve Jobs*

Apple explores music

Steve wanted to make Apple products a part of people's everyday lives. Then they would never turn their backs on the company again. His next focus was music. Apple scouts had discovered a software programme called SoundJam MP, owned by a small company called Casady and Greene (C&G), which allowed people to play MP3 files (digital music files).

Apple made C&G an offer: sell us the rights to SoundJam, or we'll develop a competitive product and put you out of business. C&G had little choice but to agree. They also lost SoundJam's original developer Jeff Robbin to Apple's in-house team. By January 2001, Apple was able to announce the launch of 'iTunes' – a simple, free download that meant Macintosh users could copy tracks from a CD onto their computer, and play them digitally.

Users could also download the files onto portable MP3 players, although sales of these devices at the time were very low. Steve decided this was because the products were badly designed, and saw another opportunity for Apple to capture a market. He hired hardware developer Tony Fadell, who based his designs on an existing product called PortalPlayer.

Apple has cool and very distinctive advertising.

> *Without the iPod, the digital music age would have been defined by files and folders instead of songs and albums. Though the medium of music has changed, the iPod experience has kept the spirit of what it means to be a music lover alive.*
>
> **John Mayer, singer and songwriter**

Apple's prototype was shrunk down, and its usability improved. Designer Jonathan Ive (see pages 24-25) oversaw the look of the new product, and on 23 October, 2001, Apple introduced its first iPod, with enough storage for 1,000 songs.

Sales gradually grew with 140,000 sold between July and September 2002, and 200,000 sold between October and Christmas. The iPod became the company's most successful product. The final part of the plan was the iTunes Music Store, announced in April 2003, which allows users to purchase and download music online. Apple's secure downloading process and payment system won over the record companies' concerns about the increased threat of piracy and illegal downloading.

The iTunes Store opened its doors with a library of 200,000 songs, each available for 99 cents (60p). Within a year, Apple had taken over 70 per cent of the legal music download business, selling 85 million songs, and the iTunes Music Store was named *Fortune* magazine's Product of the Year.

Brains Behind The Brand

Tony Fadell – former Senior Vice President of the iPod Division
A computer engineering graduate from the University of Michigan, Tony joined Apple as the first member of its iPod hardware engineering team in 2001, and is credited as the man responsible for bringing the world's most successful digital music player to market.

Tony was promoted to vice president of iPod engineering in 2004, and became senior vice president of the iPod Division in April 2006, before leaving Apple in 2008.

The invention of the iPhone

Part of the secret to any business's continued success is looking ahead to how a market might change, and how its products can stay relevant. In 2002, even before Apple released the first iPod, Steve Jobs began thinking about developing a phone. At the time, millions of people were carrying separate phones, Blackberrys for email, and MP3 players, and Steve was sure that a single device combining all three would be extremely popular.

By the summer of 2004, 3G phones (which allowed users to surf the Internet and download data at high speed) were becoming more popular, wi-fi phones were on the horizon, and rivals to the iTunes Music Store were appearing.

At the time, the iPod accounted for 16 per cent of Apple revenues, and Steve saw a danger that if another company came up with this device before Apple, the iPod's dominance as a music player would be threatened.

Steve approached handset manufacturer Motorola, and together they developed the ROKR phone, launched in September 2005. Unfortunately, the phone was a flop – it looked boring, was hard to use, and could only hold 100 songs.

The answer, Steve realised, was for Apple to design their own phone. There were numerous challenges to overcome – from developing revolutionary touchscreen technology, to rewriting a complete operating system that would make the phone work, to ensuring that the phone was safe and didn't emit dangerous levels of radiation.

After an estimated $150 million (£95 million) was spent on development, the iPhone went on sale on 29 June, 2007. In the US, Steve struck a unique deal with mobile carrier AT&T: in return for five years' exclusivity with AT&T, 10 per cent of iPhone sales in AT&T stores, and a small percentage of iTunes revenue, Apple received $10 (£6.40) per month from every iPhone customer's AT&T bill. Most importantly

An advert for the iPhone in China.

The sales of iPods and iPhones

q refers to the quarters of a business year, which is split into four quarters:
Jan-March (q1), April-June (q2), July-Sept (q3), Oct-Dec (q4).

This graph shows the sales of iPods and iPhones over a three-year period.

it retained complete control over design, manufacturing and marketing of the phone.

The iPhone was everything Steve wanted it to be, and it was a huge success. Its looks, ease of use, and great range of functions helped it sell three million handsets in the first six months, and six million in the first year. With an estimated $80 (£50) profit on every $399 (£250) phone sold, it also became Apple's most profitable product!

Business Matters

Advertising — this is a form of communication intended to persuade an audience (viewers, readers or listeners) to purchase or take some action regarding products, ideas, or services. Advertising includes the name of a product or service and how that product or service could benefit the consumer, in order to persuade the consumer to purchase that particular brand. These messages are viewed via various media — TV, print etc. Advertising can also communicate an idea to a large number of people in an attempt to convince them to take a certain action, for example to vote in an election.

There's an app for that!

The iPhone became a must-have device. But must-have devices can quickly disappear if consumers find something more interesting, or more fun, to move on to. What really kept the iPhone on top was the launch of the App Store in July 2008.

The App Store was the direct result of Apple inviting outside software developers to create applications for the iPod Touch, iPhone and most recently the iPad (see pages 22-23). The Software Development Kit (SDK) for iPhone was announced in March 2008, and allowed any developer to create applications and distribute them through the App Store on iTunes.

All applications have to pass Apple's approval process for basic reliability and suitability, and are rated based on their content regarding what age group they are suitable for. The four ratings are 4+, 7+, 12+ and 17+. Depending on the application, some

are given away free, and others cost anywhere from 0.59p to £4.99 and above. Apple take 30 per cent of any revenues generated, and pass 70 per cent to the app's developer.

The App Store was an instant success. It took Apple over three years to hit two billion song downloads from iTunes, but it took less than one and a half years to hit two billion app downloads! On the day of launch, 500 apps were available. Ten million downloads were made during the first weekend alone, and the numbers continued at a rate of half a million downloads a day, generating $1 million (£640,000) per day in revenues. As of 20 October, 2010, the number of apps in the store had grown to over 300,000!

This is the popular ➤
Angry Birds game being played on an iPad.

Not surprisingly, this had made a significant contribution to Apple's annual revenues. In June 2010, Steve Jobs announced that there had been 5 billion app downloads in two years, with Apple earning around $410 million (£260 million) from its 30 per cent cut of sales.

Brains Behind The Brand

Eddy Cue – Vice President for Internet Services

Eddy gradually became one of Steve Jobs' most trusted deputies. Eddy was given the job of creating the iTunes Store and then, alongside Steve, his role grew to negotiating with record labels and Hollywood film studios for content to fill it!

iTunes was quickly clocking up millions of downloads per week, and Eddy's next project was the App Store. He has turned it into the best-used app service on the Internet, a long way ahead of Google, Microsoft and Research In Motion, who produce the Blackberry. Eddy's next big project is tackling the eBook market, and creating a successful iBook Store for the iPad.

Business Matters

Profit and loss – a profit and loss statement is a company's financial report that indicates how the revenue (money received from the sale of products and services before expenses are taken out, also known as the 'top line') is transformed into the net income (the result after all revenues and expenses have been taken out, also known as the 'bottom line'). The revenues for a specific period are shown, and the cost and expenses charged against those revenues. The purpose of the profit and loss statement is to show company managers and investors whether the company made or lost money during the period being reported.

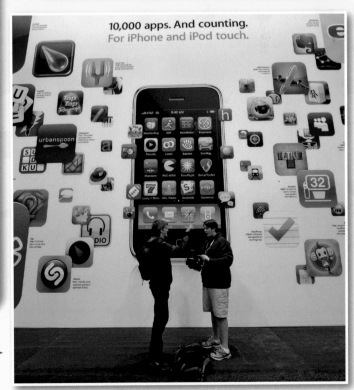

Eye-catching graphics advertise the hundreds ➤ of apps available from the App Store

Apple takes on publishing

For any company that thrives on growth, it is vitally important to keep innovating and moving forward. Apple's next decision was to start to overhaul their personal computer division. By combining the look and feel of the iPhone into a large (243 mm x 190 mm) tablet PC with a touchscreen, they were able to offer the most popular functions that computer users wanted – email, gaming, music, access to the Internet – in a device that they knew users would love.

The iPad, launched on 30 April, 2010 had actually been developed before the iPhone, but Steve Jobs decided to put it on hold and launch the iPhone first. He believed that adding a phone to the iPod Touch's range of functions would be a winner with consumers.

Weighing just 1.5 pounds (680 grams) with a 9.7-inch LCD touchscreen, the iPad sits between the smaller iPhone and the laptop. It is aimed at the games, movie and music market, and at the book, magazine and newspaper market. This has sent shockwaves through the publishing industry.

▼ *People can use the iPad to navigate their route and find out where they are going.*

> [The] iPad is... a stunningly exciting object, one that you will want now and one that will not be matched this year by any company.

Stephen Fry, TV presenter and technology enthusiast

By the launch date, Apple had built an iBookstore as part of iTunes (at the time of going to press, this is currently only available in the USA) and had agreements with major US publishers, including Penguin, Macmillan, HarperCollins and Simon & Schuster, to publish books for the iPad. Several magazines and newspapers, including *GQ*, *Vanity Fair*, *Wired* and *The New York Times* have also released iPad versions.

It's too early to tell whether the iPad will cause the death or the rebirth of publishing, but it has already helped increase publishers' sales. Because Apple only takes a 30 per cent cut from eBook sales through iTunes, the other great online retailer Amazon has been forced to reduce its own cut of book sales from 50 per cent down to 30 per cent to stay competitive. The iPad has also proved a huge success with consumers. By selling 7.5 million units in its first five months, it became the fastest selling consumer electronics device in history – faster than the iPhone and even the DVD player! Forecasts predict 28 million sales in 2011.

Business Matters

Diversification — companies often decide to offer new products or services, like the iPhone and the App Store, because it reduces the risk of its other products becoming too limited or uninteresting. By adding new products to its range, Apple gives consumers more reasons to buy Apple products. When companies offer a completely different product or service, like supermarkets offering car or house insurance, this is called 'brandstretching'.

You can watch and read the news on an iPad.

What makes Apple products so 'must-have'?

If there is one secret ingredient, one USP (Unique Selling Proposition or Point) behind Apple's success it is their understanding of the importance of good design. From the Apple I in 1976 right up to the iPad in 2010, each and every one of Apple's products has been built to look great, and to stand apart as iconic timeless designs. The hope is that consumers will love to look at them, just as much as they love to use them.

Apple are fortunate to have an award-winning designer, Jonathan Ive (see box on page 25) as their Head of Industrial Design. According to Jonathan, they are just as lucky to have a CEO like Steve Jobs, who is 'an exceptional designer' and shares Jonathan's love of excellent design.

Together, Jonathan and Steve are held responsible for Apple's ability to delight and dazzle consumers with their famous products, from the brightly coloured iMac, that changed people's perceptions of what a PC should look like, to the tiny iPod Nano and iPod Shuffle.

So how can Apple create mass-produced products that look like they were made by hand? In a 1996 interview, Steve said, 'Design is a funny word. Some people think design means how [a product] looks. But, of course, if you dig deeper, it's really how [a product] works. To design something really well, you have to "get it".'

Jonathan agrees. He puts his success down to limiting the number of projects he works on, caring deeply about the products he designs, and focusing only on what's important, and what will make a product stand out as different.

For his outstanding design work, Jonathan was named 'the most influential person in British culture' for 2004, beating Harry Potter author JK Rowling!

To create a plastic shell for the first iMac, and to make it look exciting rather than cheap, Jonathan and his team spent time in a sweet factory studying how jelly beans were made! They then spent months in Asia with manufacturers, producing case after case until they found a way to make millions every year to the same high standards. They even requested that the internal electronics be redesigned so that they looks nicer through the see-through casing. With dedication like that, it's not hard to see why Apple is regarded as the most design-oriented company in the world.

> From early on, we wanted a product that would seem so natural and so inevitable and so simple, you almost wouldn't think of it as having been designed.
>
> **Jonathan Ive, on the iPod**

The Nano has become one of Apple's most popular products.

Brains Behind The Brand

Jonathan Ive – Senior Vice President for Industrial Design
Jonathan was hired by Apple in 1992. When Steve Jobs returned to Apple and closed down production on all but four of Apple's 60 products, he started to search for a design superstar to rejuvenate Apple's product line. Jonathan expected to lose his job. Instead, Steve realised the genius he was looking for was right under his nose, and put Jonathan in charge!

The pair's success started with the first iMac, and now includes the iPod, iPhone, iPad, MacBook Air and many more products.

What does the future hold for Apple?

Apple has built a fantastic reputation for innovation, style and fun. Steve Jobs and his team seem to second guess what consumers want, even before we know we want it!

Although no one apart from Steve and his most trusted employees really know what Apple's plans are for the next ten years, it's fair to assume the company will continue to focus on entertainment – specifically, music, movies, games and television. And here's the evidence.

Firstly, Apple's hold on the handheld gaming market was up 53.2 per cent in 2010 from the previous year, with 43.8 per cent of gamers playing on the iPhone and iPod Touch rather than the Nintendo DS and Sony PSP.

The much-anticipated iPad 2 (7.3 inches wide) launched in 2011 and suggests a move by Apple to strengthen their hold on this market.

Secondly, Apple are trying various tactics to give their music sales a boost. iTunes will soon be offering 90-second instead of 30-second sample clips of songs. Plus amazing deals like offering The Beatles' back catalogue for the first time on iTunes also generates huge amounts of traffic. Over two million singles, and 450,000 albums were downloaded in the first seven days!

▼ *The Beatles' albums finally became available on iTunes in 2010.*

Thirdly, a Mac App Store will launch in early 2011, to boost revenues in the desktop computer market. And, last but not least, Apple has plans to take over your living room!

Apple TV was launched just before Christmas in 2010. For under £100, this matt black 10 cm squared box allows users to rent standard and HD films through iTunes and play them on your TV; play your iTunes library through your TV speakers; listen to Podcasts and visit websites like YouTube and Flickr; and stream TV shows over the Internet. Apple TV is a little ahead of its time, and is unlikely to become the next iPod or iPhone overnight, but it shows clearly where Apple are looking – to the future of entertainment! And who would bet on them not finding another world-changing product in the next few years?

> " The resurrection of Apple is the most astounding story that's happened in business in at least a decade. You might be able to go further and say a half-century. It's on par with [the inventions of] Thomas Edison and Alexander Graham Bell in terms of its total impact. "
>
> **Technology expert Roger Kay**

Steve Jobs launches Apple TV in 2010.

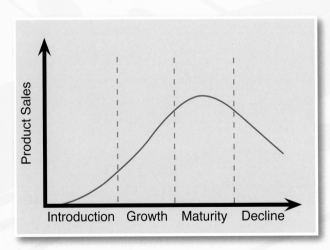

The graph above shows the natural growth and decline cycle for any product, for example the iMac, iPod and iPhone. It clearly shows the reason why Apple needs to keep innovating, and introducing great new products!

Design your own app for the App Store!

To create a new product, it is helpful to put together a product development brief like the one below. This is a sample brief for the Space Hopper app.

The SWOT analysis on the page opposite can help you to think about the strengths, weaknessess, opportunities and threats of your product. This can let you see how feasible and practical your idea is before you think of investing in it.

Product Development Brief

Name of application : Space Hopper

Design of logo

The product explained (use 25 words or less): The fun never stops! Shake your phone to bounce. Keep bouncing over bigger and bigger obstacles to win points. Great low-tech entertainment.

Target age of users: 5-100

What does the product do? Space Hopper is a simple platform game that allows iPhone owners to use the motion-sensor on their phone to activate the game's 'bounces'. It is simple and addictive.

Are there any similar products already available? Lots – games like Angry Birds and Doodle Jump are very popular, and have no difficult skills to master, or rules to learn.

What makes your product different? Space Hopper could be the next big game. It combines an element of nostalgia for older iPhone users, but is very simple and fun so kids will enjoy it too.

Name of App Store application you are assessing ... Space Hopper
The information below will help you assess your App Store application. By addressing all four areas, you can make your application stronger, and more likely to be a success.

Questions to consider	Strengths
Does your application do something unique? Is there anything innovative about it? What are its USPs (unique selling points)? Why will people use this application instead of a different application?	*The Space Hopper game has novelty value, and will attract older users who remember playing on real Space Hoppers when they were children.* *It uses the iPhone's motion sensor to make the Space Hopper bounce, therefore it is very easy to use for people of all ages.*
Why wouldn't people use this application? Does it do everything it says it can? Is it as good or better than other similar applications already available? Do you have a technical support team in place in case people have problems with the application?	**Weaknesses** *It is a new game from a brand-new developer so we have to start building users from scratch, against other much more well-established app manufacturers.* *If you are shaking your iPhone to make the Space Hopper bounce, it is not always easy to see the phone screen and avoid obstacles.*
Can the application be improved in the future, eg more features added? Will new markets emerge for this application? Can the application target new 'niche' (ie small, specific) markets? Can it be used globally? Can it develop new USPs?	**Opportunities** *Could look great and be even more fun on an iPad.* *Research may show that Space Hoppers were also popular in other countries, therefore increasing the market for the app.* *There is no language element to the game, so it can easily be played internationally.*
Is the market for applications shrinking? Will new technology make your application unnecessary? Are any of your weaknesses so bad they might affect the application in the long run? Is Apple likely to decide to remove applications from their site?	**Threats** *As Space Hoppers are not a new invention, another company may produce a better game using the same idea.* *People will get bored playing one single game, and want something new. For the company's continued success, we will need to develop more games.*

Do you have what it takes to work at Apple? Try this!

1) When you look at a computer, do you think:
a) Great, what's on YouTube?
b) I wish I had an iMac – in blue to match my bedroom.
c) If the screen was flatter, and the keyboard was built into the hard drive, this would look pretty cool!

2) If you were asked to redesign the iPod, would you say:
a) No chance, just let me listen to it!
b) Well, I'd like a touchscreen that doesn't show fingerprints.
c) Great! I've got 20 ideas already.

3) You're given a pencil and paper, and asked to create something new. Do you:
a) Write your name in bubble writing.
b) Draw your favourite cartoon of Mr Tomkins, the science teacher.
c) Create a new design for a music player that fits inside wireless headphones.

4) When you buy a pair of trainers, what do you look for?
a) I don't – my mum buys them for me.
b) I like to have what's popular at the time.
c) I spend a lot of time assessing design and performance. They need to look good and feel good.

5) Name one product you would love to own
a) A never-ending packet of salt and vinegar crisps.
b) I want a flatscreen TV for my bedroom!
c) The Alessi 'Juicy Salif' lemon squeezer would be brilliant.

6) Who is your favourite designer?
a) Do Nike and Adidas count?
b) After reading this book, it's got to be Jonathan Ive!
c) Ettore Sottsass – he designed everything from typewriters to buildings.

7) Whenever Apple launches a new product, do you think:
a) Have they launched a cheaper iPod yet?
b) Excellent – something for my Christmas list!
c) I'd love to get behind the scenes and see the thought processes that went in to making that.

Results

Mostly As: Sorry, but your chance of working at Apple is looking shaky! It doesn't sound like you have the interest in design to succeed at this world-famous company.

Mostly Bs: You're aware of design, but you need to give it more time and attention if you want to succeed in a design-led business.

Mostly Cs: It sounds like you have what it takes to get a job at Apple! Keep working hard at school, and pushing to be the best and who knows?

application   a computer program designed to help people perform a specific activity, for example word processing.

arrogant   someone who shows a high opinion of their own importance and abilities.

axing   closing down, terminating.

binary code   a system of numbers, only using 0s and 1s, which gives a computer 'instructions' on what to do.

chaotic   badly organised or confused.

circuit board   this holds all the electronic parts that go into a computer.

component   a part of something, in this case a computer, that goes into making the whole. For example, the screen and the keyboard are components.

corporate culture   the way a company is run.

emit   to give off or send out.

facilitate   to assist the progress of.

high-resolution graphics   high-quality images, in this case on a computer. The higher the resolution, the more image detail you see.

hobbyist   a term for someone who pursues something for pleasure.

innovation   something newly introduced, like a new piece of technology or a new way of doing something.

must-have device   something that looks and works so well that everyone wants to own one.

operating system   the program that runs your computer and makes it work.

radiation   energy that is transmitted or spread in the form of rays or waves or particles. Ionizing radiation can be dangerous and cause cancer.

retailer   a company that sells goods in small quantities to consumers.

revenue   a company's income before costs are taken into account; gross income.

scout   a person sent out to gain information.

Silicon Valley   an area in northern California close to San Francisco that is home to the world's largest technology companies.

spreadsheet   a program used in accountancy, which can track finances either in a company or in a single home.

tablet PC   a flat screen, handheld PC with a touch-screen keyboard.

techie   a term to describe someone who has high levels of ability in computer programming.

telecommunications   the science of communication through telephones, radio, television and so on.

thrive   to do well, prosper.